DESTINATION:
MARS

SEYMOUR SIMON

HarperCollins*Publishers*

PHOTO CREDITS:
Permission to use the following photographs is gratefully acknowledged: page 4, Richard Dreiser, The
Yerkes Observatory; pages 16–17, National Space Science Data Center and The Mars Global Surveyor
Project, The Planetary Data System; pages 18, 19, Malin Space Science Systems/NASA. All other
photographs courtesy of Jet Propulsion Laboratory (California Institute of Technology)/NASA.

Destination Mars

Printed in Singapore at Tien Wah Press.

http://www.harperchildrens.com

Library of Congress Cataloging-in-Publication Data
Simon, Seymour.
[Mars]
Destination, Mars / Seymour Simon.
p. cm.
Originally published: Mars. New York: William Morrow, c1987.
ISBN 0-688-15770-X (trade)—ISBN 0-688-15771-8 (library)
1. Mars (Planet) Juvenile literature.   I. Title.   QB641.S494 2000   523.43—dc21   99-15523   CIP

1 2 3 4 5 6 7 8 9 10
❖
First Edition

To Jeanette Carlson,

with many thanks for her assistance

Mars looks like one of the brightest stars in the night sky. But Mars is not a star; it is a planet. Mars appears so bright because it is closer to us on Earth than any other planet except Venus.

Mars is sometimes called the red planet because iron oxide (rust) in the soil makes it shine with a reddish or orange color. Two thousand years ago, the red color made the Romans think of blood and war. So they named the planet Mars, after their god of war.

Mars is the fourth planet from the sun, after Mercury, Venus, and our own planet, Earth. Mars is more than 140 million miles from the sun—50 million miles farther away from the sun than Earth. It is also a smaller planet than Earth, 4,218 miles across. If Earth were hollow, seven planets the size of Mars could fit inside.

Earth and Mars travel around the sun in paths called orbits. Earth takes one year—365 days—to orbit the sun. But Mars is farther away and takes longer to orbit the sun. A Martian year is 687 Earth days, almost twice as long as a year on Earth. A Martian day is only about half an hour longer than a day on Earth.

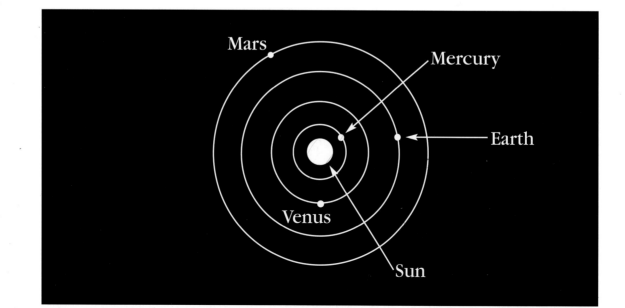

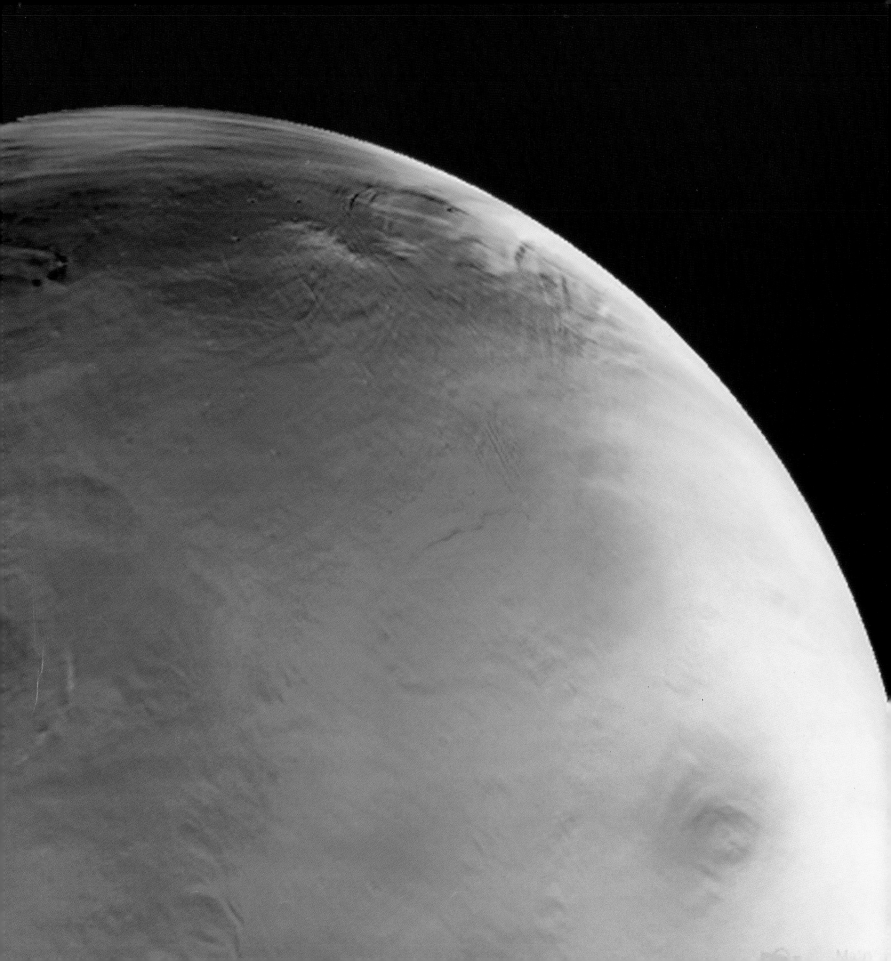

About one hundred years ago, an Italian astronomer named Giovanni Schiaparelli studied Mars through a telescope. He imagined he saw many straight, dark lines on the surface of the planet. He called them *canali*, the Italian word for *channels*, but some people thought he meant *canals*.

People heard about the "canals" on Mars. Since they knew that canals are waterways dug by people, they decided that intelligent Martians must have made the canals. Some astronomers drew maps of Mars showing canals crisscrossing the planet.

People began to imagine all kinds of things living on Mars. In 1898, H. G. Wells's book *The War of the Worlds* described tentacled, bug-eyed Martians trying to conquer Earth. Forty years later, a radio play by Orson Welles had Martians invading New Jersey. Thousands of people, believing that the story was real, fled their homes in terror. Since then, there have been many

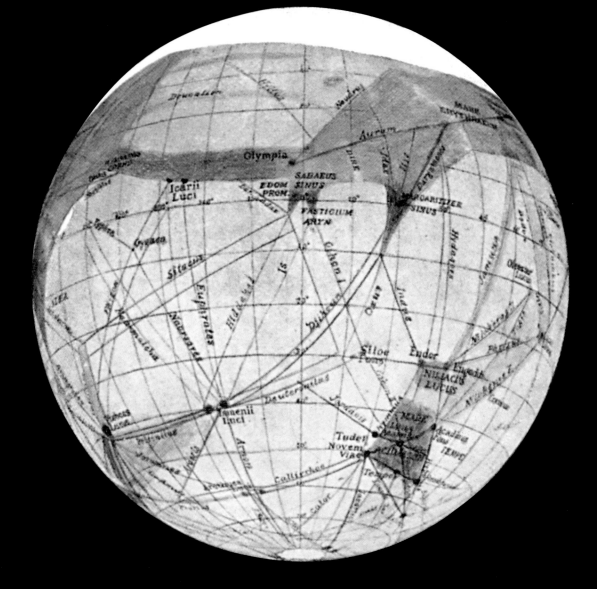

science-fiction books, movies, and television programs about invaders from Mars.

Neither the *Viking* spacecraft launched in the 1970s nor the *Pathfinder* spacecraft of the 1990s found any canals, or any life at all, on the planet. But scientists still are not sure whether life existed on Mars in the past.

This view of Mars was sent back to Earth from one of the *Viking* spacecraft. It shows that the Martian surface has craters, mountains, volcanoes, plains, and valleys—but no straight lines. No one knows what the earlier astronomers were seeing when they thought they saw "canals." At the bottom of the photo, you can see the curving line of Mars's biggest valley, Valles Marineris, which stretches for almost three thousand miles across the surface of the planet.

Mars has cooled down, but it was once very hot inside, as Earth was in the past and still is. Molten rock, called lava, erupted out on the surface, building huge volcanic peaks.

This is Olympus Mons, the largest known volcano on any planet of the Solar System. The *Mars Global Surveyor* spacecraft reached Mars in September 1997 and took the photo during one of its orbits around the planet that year.

Olympus Mons rises fifteen miles into the air. This is almost three times as high as Mount Everest, the highest mountain on Earth. The steep base of the volcano would cover the entire state of Missouri. The collapsed center is fifty miles across. Olympus Mons is one of four giant volcanoes in a group just north of the Martian equator.

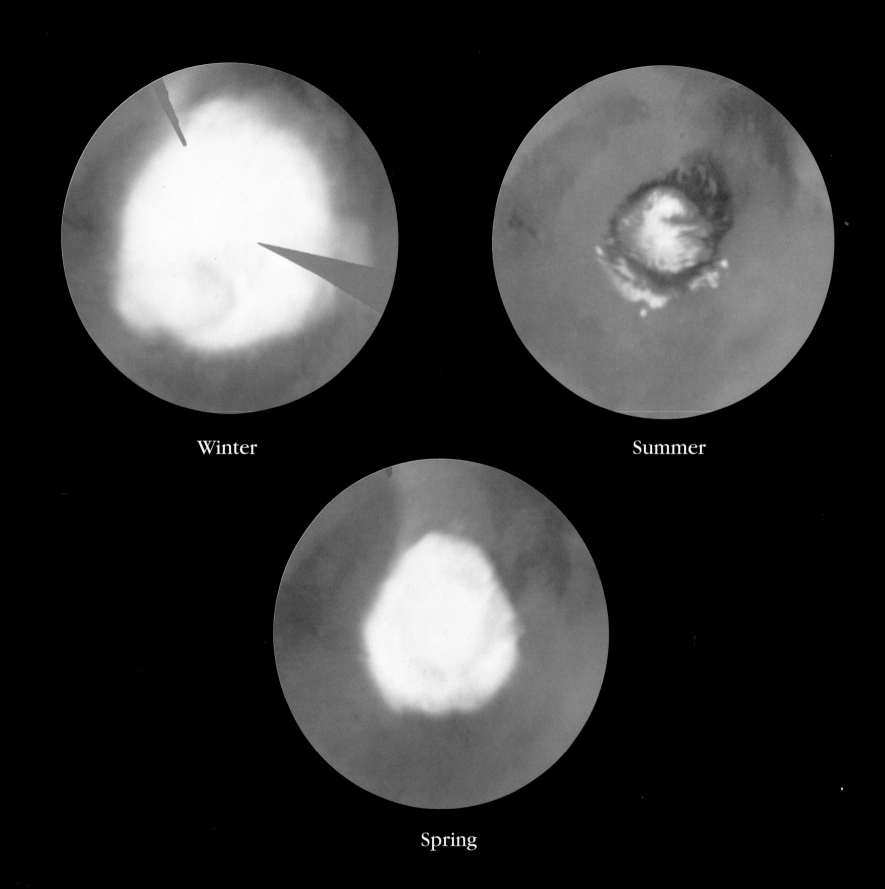

Winter

Summer

Spring

NASA's Hubble Space Telescope (HST) took these images of the north polar ice cap over the course of a Martian year. They show the seasonal changes that take place in the size of the ice cap from the Martian winter (upper left) to spring (middle) to summer (upper right). Other color changes shown in the photographs are the result of dust storms that hide or reveal darker materials on the surface.

The north polar ice cap is composed mostly of water ice, just like Earth's polar ice caps. It has an average thickness of about six-tenths of a mile and covers an area one and a half times the size of Texas. The Martian polar cap has much less ice than either of Earth's ice caps—only about 4 percent of the amount in the Antarctic ice sheet, for instance.

Surveyor sends laser pulses toward the planet and measures the time it takes for them to bounce back. Scientists used these measurements to make this three-dimensional photograph and a map of Mars's North Pole in 1998.

The Martian ice cap has canyons that plunge as much as three thousand feet beneath the surface. The canyons are formed by winds cutting through the ice and by the evaporation of water into the atmosphere.

Scientists believe that an ancient ocean with ten times the amount of water in the ice cap once existed on Mars. They think that the remaining water not in the north polar ice cap is stored below the surface and in the much smaller south polar cap, or else it has been lost into space.

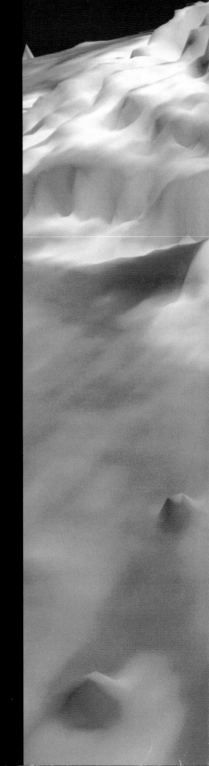

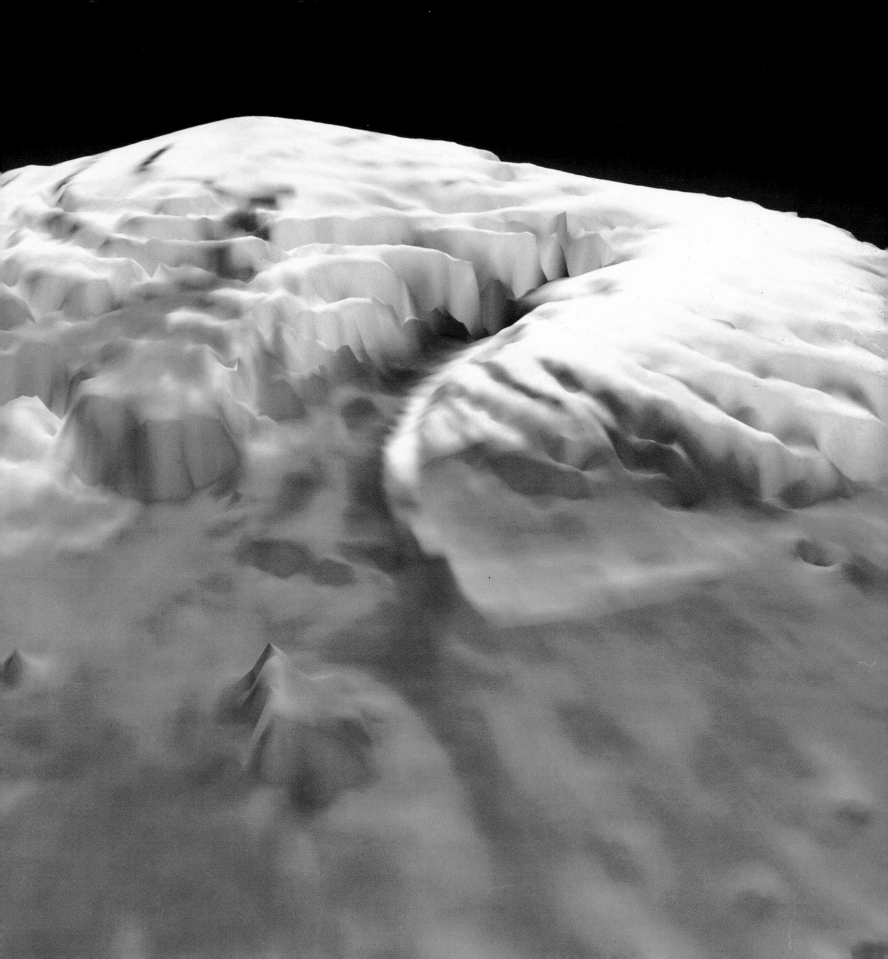

The Mars Orbiter Camera carried aboard the *Mars Global Surveyor* spacecraft took this close-up image of Martian sand dunes in 1998. Parts of the dunes are covered by bright frost, but in some places the frost has melted, revealing the dark sand below. The sand has been blown in streaks over the frost. This shows that despite the thin atmosphere of Mars, wind still blows the dunes. Martian air at the surface of the planet is about one hundred times thinner than Earth's air at sea level.

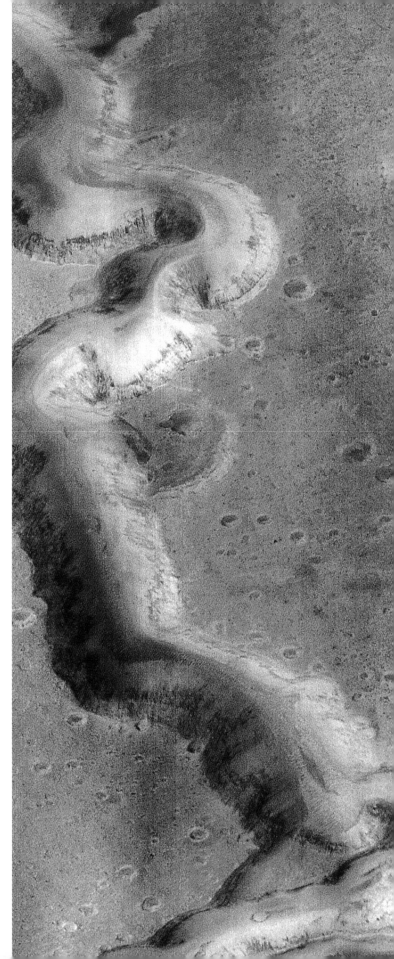

These canyons on Mars were photographed by the Mars Orbiter Camera in 1998. They show layers of different kinds of rocks. One day these rocks may help scientists who travel to Mars understand the history of the planet. This system of canyons and troughs is part of Mars's biggest valley, Valles Marineris. Four times as deep as Arizona's Grand Canyon, the valley would stretch from Los Angeles to New York if it occurred on Earth.

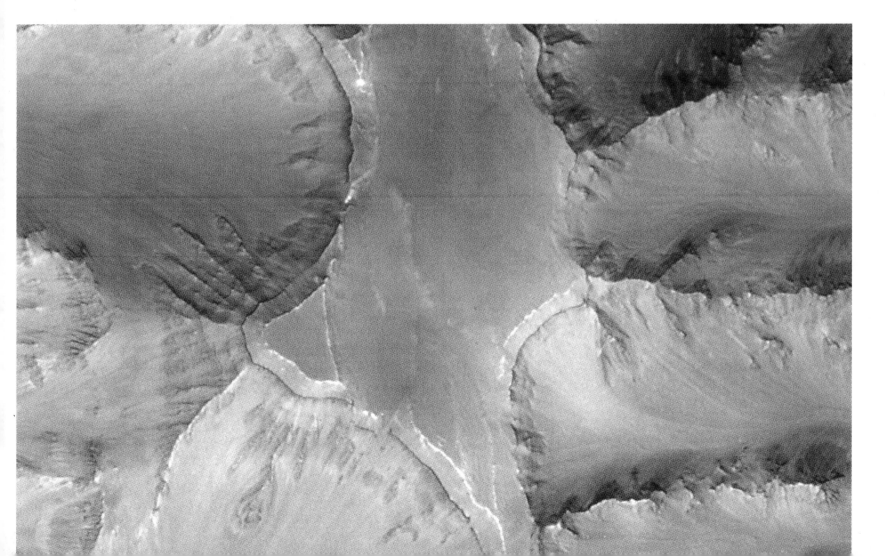

Phobos

Mars has two small moons, Phobos and Deimos. They are named after the two sons of Ares, the Greek god of war. Phobos [FO-bos] is the larger of the two moons and nearer to Mars. Phobos is about seventeen miles long and twelve miles wide. It races around Mars in only seven and one-half hours, at a distance of about 3,000 miles from the planet. If you were an observer on Mars, Phobos would look several times brighter than a very bright star does from Earth. The close-up photo of Phobos shows large meteorite craters and deep scratches across the surface.

Deimos [DIE-mos] is slightly smaller than Phobos, about nine miles long by seven miles wide. Deimos takes a bit longer than thirty hours to orbit Mars and is about 12,500 miles away from the planet. From the surface of Mars, Deimos would look as bright as the planet Venus does from Earth.

Deimos

On December 4, 1996, the Mars *Pathfinder* was launched from the Kennedy Space Center in Florida. Aboard the spaceship was a lander and a small six-wheeled rover called Sojourner.

The *Pathfinder* spaceship took seven months to reach Mars and go into orbit around it. On July 4, 1997, the *Pathfinder* lander touched down on the surface of the planet. Air bags inflated to cushion the landing.

The lander bounced about fifty feet into the air, then bounced another fifteen times up and down before coming to rest. The impact area was named the Sagan Memorial Station, after Carl Sagan, an American astronomer who had been very interested in the exploration of Mars.

Sojourner is the first robot rover to explore Mars. It weighs about twenty-four pounds on Earth (only about nine pounds on Mars) and is about the size of a child's toy wagon. It can move at speeds up to about two feet per minute. Even though this isn't very fast, Sojourner was able to accomplish many tasks during a Martian day.

Based on the discoveries of the *Pathfinder* lander and rover, scientists think that Mars was once much more like Earth is now, with an ocean and rivers and a thicker atmosphere.

P*athfinder* has sent back to Earth more than sixteen thousand photographs, more than fifteen chemical analyses of rocks, and much information on winds and other weather factors. This data has helped scientists make many important discoveries about Mars. The rocks

and pebbles suggest that some were formed when Mars was warmer and wetter. Mars is now a dusty planet, lacking in liquid water on the surface. The atmosphere is very clear, but there are frequent "dust devils," wind gusts that swirl dust into the air.

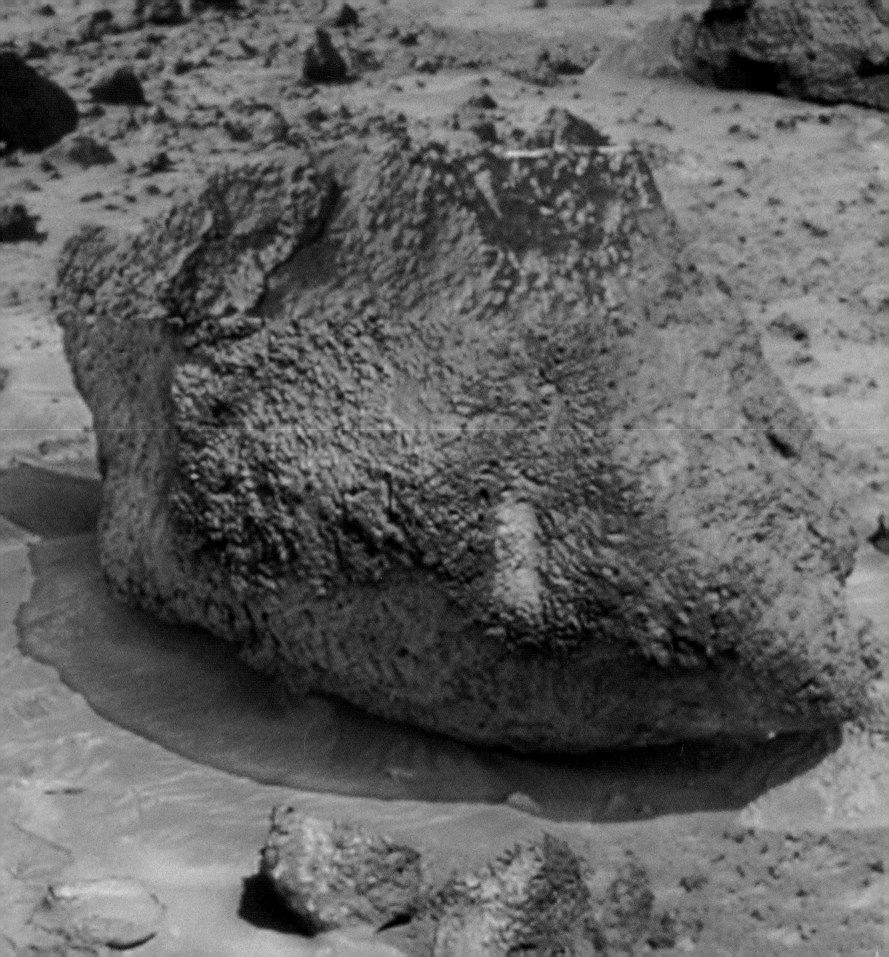

Is there life on Mars? So far, no one knows for sure. The *Viking* landers of 1976 found no trace of life in the soil. But in 1996, scientists announced the discovery of possible evidence of life inside a meteorite that came from Mars and collided with Earth about thirteen thousand years ago. Minerals in the meteorite suggest that some kind of microscopic life may have existed on Mars more than three billion years ago.

Mars is a harsh planet for human life. The pressure of the atmosphere is so low that your blood would boil if you stepped out on the surface without a space suit. You'd also have to dress very warmly. The temperature is much colder than a deep freeze both day and night.

On the other hand, the pull of gravity on the surface of the planet is so low that you could easily walk around in a space suit. If you weigh one hundred pounds on Earth, you would weigh only thirty-eight pounds on Mars.

Over the next few years, many other spacecraft are set to find out more about Mars:

- The *Mars Climate Orbiter*, launched in late 1998, will study the planet's weather and serve as a radio relay for future Mars missions.

- The *Mars Polar Lander*, launched on January 3, 1999, will touch down near Mars's South Pole and look for water in the soil.

- In 2001, the *Mars 2001 Surveyor and Lander* will further study the makeup of the planet.

- In 2003, NASA will begin a series of missions, some of which are designed to bring Martian rocks and soil samples back to Earth by 2008.

- In 2005, NASA and CNES, the French space agency, will launch an orbiter, lander, and rover. The rover will collect samples, which will then be rocketed into orbit. The orbiter will retrieve the samples and return them to Earth.

- From 2007 to 2013, additional sampling missions will be launched every two years.

The *Pathfinder* lander took these images of a Martian sunset. Because there is so much dust in the air, the sunsets are spectacular and last for an hour. We've learned so much about the once-feared red planet that someone reading this now may set foot on the surface of